RELEASED

SET IN SOUL

THIS JOURNAL BELONGS TO

_____

DEDICATED TO EVERYTHING THAT BELONGS
TO ME. I'M STARTING TO LET GO.

TABLE OF CONTENTS

HOW TO USE THIS JOURNAL

In this journal titled Released, the goal is to let go of any habit that you feel is preventing you from being your best self. The best way to get rid of a negative habit is to replace it with a positive one. Whether it's a habit you picked up when you were younger or a habit you picked up out of convenience, comfort, or curiosity, you will find that ALL habits can be replaced. With self-discipline, consistency and prayer, you will witness your life transform not just from releasing old habits but also from gaining strength and self-confidence from this experience. It's easy to believe that you cannot develop the self-discipline, consistency or prayer muscles that is needed to break unwanted habits because your mind has gotten comfortable with its well-established routine and thoughts. But with the help of this journal, a reprogramming of your mind is possible. Your thoughts will now work in your best interest rather than against you. You know it is possible to be released from old habits, and that is why this journal now belongs to you. You will not only figure out the whys but also remove yourself from the emotional attachment of putting bad habits into practice.

Like all habits, it will take time to make it a regular part of your life. It is said that it takes 30 days to practice and form a new habit. Others say it takes 67 days for it to stick. This journal covers 150 days, about five months. It is important to dedicate this time to yourself and write in this journal daily to establish, track, and report your progress. What makes creating a new habit effortless? Repetition. It takes doing something over and over again, even when you don't feel like it or when it's an inconvenience or a challenge for it to stick. The prompts in this journal are repetitive on purpose. Each day is a different day to reinforce your goal, reprogram your mind, and stay focused. Throughout this journal, you will find motivational quotes to keep you going. It is recommended that you fill out this journal toward the beginning of your day and review it at night. You will likely make some mistakes along the way, but this is the time to be gentle with yourself and pick yourself back up with a positive attitude. This is your place to release habits that no longer belong in your space and form new habits that will help you be the best version of yourself.

So let's get started.

THESE OLD HABITS

THESE OLD HABITS

What Do I Want?

What Do I Need?

What Have I Been Doing That Is Currently Hurting Me?

What Am I Doing For Others That Is Not Helpful To Me?

THESE OLD HABITS

What Kind Of Conversations Do I Partake In That Do Not Help Me To Grow?

What Activities Do I Need To Stop Partaking In?

In The Past, I Have Done _____ Because

_____.

I Notice There Is A Pattern In:

The People Around Me:

THESE OLD HABITS

I Know I Must:

Negative Habits I Have Been Trying To Let Go Of:

I Started These Habits Because:

The Only Thing These Habits Have Done For Me:

These Habits Have Caused Me To:

THESE OLD HABITS

These Habits Have Formed These Other Habits:

What Makes This Habit So Hard To Break (Write The Strongest Habit You Want To Break):

What Has To Change To Break This Habit?

Who Motivates Me To Break This Habit?

My Bad Habits Do Not Only Affect Me, But They Also Have An Impact On:

THESE OLD HABITS

My Old Habits Are Costing Me:

As A Result Of My Old Habits, I:

I Have Relied On My Old Habits So Much Because:

My Old Habits Made Me Feel:

My Old Habits Protected Me From:

THESE OLD HABITS

My Old Habits Have Caused Me To:

My Old Habits Exposed Me To:

My Old Mindset Was:

I Picked Up These Old Habits From:

I Have Learned:

THESE OLD HABITS

What Triggers My Negative Habits?

I Feel Like _____ After I _____.

What Caused The Above Feeling?

Some Of The Excuses I Make For My Habits:

Before Acting On My Negative Habits, I Feel And Think:

THESE OLD HABITS

The New Thought (Towards Myself And My Habits) That I Will Replace
My Old Thoughts With:

The Steps I Am Taking To Break These Unwanted Habits:

THESE NEW
HABITS

THESE NEW HABITS

My Goal Is:

I Have Made The Decision To:

My New Next Level Looks Like:

I Am Excited Because:

I Believe I Can:

THESE NEW HABITS

Before This Seemed Impossible:

But Now I Know I Can:

My Daily Affirmation Will Be:

I Currently Feel:

I Am Determined To Establish These Habits (List Them):

THESE NEW HABITS

These New Habits Will Make Me Feel:

I Am Capable Of Forming These New Habits Because I Am:

My New Mindset:

My New Thoughts Towards My New Habits Are:

To Form These New Habits, It Will Require:

THESE NEW HABITS

The Experiences I Want To Have:

My New Daily Routine Looks Like:

I Know That Being Consistent Means:

I Am Not Afraid Of:

This Change In My Life Will Affect:

THESE NEW HABITS

In The Past, I Have Always Wanted To:

I Will No Longer Be Dependent On:

I Will Now Depend On:

My New Rule Is:

My Weakness Is:

THESE NEW HABITS

But My Strength Is:

I Will Practice:

I Will Treat Myself When:

A Daily Compliment To Myself Will Be:

People Who Inspire Me To Create My New Habits And Stick To Them:

THESE NEW HABITS

My New Habits Will Help Me:

What I Am Currently Doing That Is Helping Me:

I Am Willing To _____ So I Can

_____.

A NEW WAY
OF LIVING

A NEW WAY OF LIVING

Date: Mood: Days Into New Habit:

The New Habit I Am Forming/Working On:

I Am Motivated By:

I Plan On Forming This New Habit Today By:

I Am Noticing:

I Am Letting Go Of The Old Feeling Of:

Despite How I Feel, I Will:

As I Start Working On My New Habit Today, I Will Feel:

I Look Forward To:

I Am Making Room For This New Habit In My Life By:

Today I Am Asking Myself:

Today I Will Set My Intention On:

The Answer To My Question Above Is:

I Am Maintaining The Positive Habits I Currently Have By:

A NEW WAY OF LIVING

Date: Mood: Days Into New Habit:

The New Habit I Am Forming/Working
On:

I Am Motivated By:

I Plan On Forming This New Habit Today
By:

I Am Noticing:

I Am Letting Go Of The Old Feeling Of:

Despite How I Feel, I Will:

As I Start Working On My New Habit
Today, I Will Feel:

I Look Forward To:

I Am Making Room For This New Habit In
My Life By:

Today I Am Asking Myself:

Today I Will Set My Intention On:

The Answer To My Question Above Is:

I Am Maintaining The Positive Habits I
Currently Have By:

A NEW WAY OF LIVING

Date: Mood: Days Into New Habit:

The New Habit I Am Forming/Working On:

I Am Motivated By:

I Plan On Forming This New Habit Today By:

I Am Noticing:

I Am Letting Go Of The Old Feeling Of:

Despite How I Feel, I Will:

As I Start Working On My New Habit Today, I Will Feel:

I Look Forward To:

I Am Making Room For This New Habit In My Life By:

Today I Am Asking Myself:

Today I Will Set My Intention On:

The Answer To My Question Above Is:

I Am Maintaining The Positive Habits I Currently Have By:

I AM COMMITTED TO ME.

MY RELEASED THOUGHTS

A NEW WAY OF LIVING

Date: Mood: Days Into New Habit:

The New Habit I Am Forming/Working On: | I Am Motivated By:

I Plan On Forming This New Habit Today By: | I Am Noticing:

I Am Letting Go Of The Old Feeling Of: | Despite How I Feel, I Will:

As I Start Working On My New Habit Today, I Will Feel: | I Look Forward To:

I Am Making Room For This New Habit In My Life By: | Today I Am Asking Myself:

Today I Will Set My Intention On: | The Answer To My Question Above Is:

I Am Maintaining The Positive Habits I Currently Have By:

A NEW WAY OF LIVING

Date: Mood: Days Into New Habit:

The New Habit I Am Forming/Working On:

I Am Motivated By:

I Plan On Forming This New Habit Today By:

I Am Noticing:

I Am Letting Go Of The Old Feeling Of:

Despite How I Feel, I Will:

As I Start Working On My New Habit Today, I Will Feel:

I Look Forward To:

I Am Making Room For This New Habit In My Life By:

Today I Am Asking Myself:

Today I Will Set My Intention On:

The Answer To My Question Above Is:

I Am Maintaining The Positive Habits I Currently Have By:

A NEW WAY OF LIVING

Date: Mood: Days Into New Habit:

The New Habit I Am Forming/Working On:

I Am Motivated By:

I Plan On Forming This New Habit Today By:

I Am Noticing:

I Am Letting Go Of The Old Feeling Of:

Despite How I Feel, I Will:

As I Start Working On My New Habit Today, I Will Feel:

I Look Forward To:

I Am Making Room For This New Habit In My Life By:

Today I Am Asking Myself:

Today I Will Set My Intention On:

The Answer To My Question Above Is:

I Am Maintaining The Positive Habits I Currently Have By:

MY BEST HABIT.....

MY RELEASED
THOUGHTS

A NEW WAY OF LIVING

Date: Mood: Days Into New Habit:

The New Habit I Am Forming/Working On:

I Am Motivated By:

I Plan On Forming This New Habit Today By:

I Am Noticing:

I Am Letting Go Of The Old Feeling Of:

Despite How I Feel, I Will:

As I Start Working On My New Habit Today, I Will Feel:

I Look Forward To:

I Am Making Room For This New Habit In My Life By:

Today I Am Asking Myself:

Today I Will Set My Intention On:

The Answer To My Question Above Is:

I Am Maintaining The Positive Habits I Currently Have By:

A NEW WAY OF LIVING

Date: Mood: Days Into New Habit:

The New Habit I Am Forming/Working On:

I Am Motivated By:

I Plan On Forming This New Habit Today By:

I Am Noticing:

I Am Letting Go Of The Old Feeling Of:

Despite How I Feel, I Will:

As I Start Working On My New Habit Today, I Will Feel:

I Look Forward To:

I Am Making Room For This New Habit In My Life By:

Today I Am Asking Myself:

Today I Will Set My Intention On:

The Answer To My Question Above Is:

I Am Maintaining The Positive Habits I Currently Have By:

A NEW WAY OF LIVING

Date: Mood: Days Into New Habit:

The New Habit I Am Forming/Working On:

I Am Motivated By:

I Plan On Forming This New Habit Today By:

I Am Noticing:

I Am Letting Go Of The Old Feeling Of:

Despite How I Feel, I Will:

As I Start Working On My New Habit Today, I Will Feel:

I Look Forward To:

I Am Making Room For This New Habit In My Life By:

Today I Am Asking Myself:

Today I Will Set My Intention On:

The Answer To My Question Above Is:

I Am Maintaining The Positive Habits I Currently Have By:

A NEW WAY OF LIVING

Date: Mood: Days Into New Habit:

The New Habit I Am Forming/Working On: I Am Motivated By:

I Plan On Forming This New Habit Today By: I Am Noticing:

I Am Letting Go Of The Old Feeling Of: Despite How I Feel, I Will:

As I Start Working On My New Habit Today, I Will Feel: I Look Forward To:

I Am Making Room For This New Habit In My Life By: Today I Am Asking Myself:

Today I Will Set My Intention On: The Answer To My Question Above Is:

I Am Maintaining The Positive Habits I Currently Have By:

I WILL NOT BE CONFINED BY MY OLD THOUGHTS. I WILL NOT BE CONFINED BY MY OLD WAYS.

I AM
EMBRACING
THIS
CHANGE.

A NEW WAY OF LIVING

Date: Mood: Days Into New Habit:

The New Habit I Am Forming/Working On: | I Am Motivated By:

I Plan On Forming This New Habit Today By: | I Am Noticing:

I Am Letting Go Of The Old Feeling Of: | Despite How I Feel, I Will:

As I Start Working On My New Habit Today, I Will Feel: | I Look Forward To:

I Am Making Room For This New Habit In My Life By: | Today I Am Asking Myself:

Today I Will Set My Intention On: | The Answer To My Question Above Is:

I Am Maintaining The Positive Habits I Currently Have By:

A NEW WAY OF LIVING

Date: Mood: Days Into New Habit:

The New Habit I Am Forming/Working On:

I Am Motivated By:

I Plan On Forming This New Habit Today By:

I Am Noticing:

I Am Letting Go Of The Old Feeling Of:

Despite How I Feel, I Will:

As I Start Working On My New Habit Today, I Will Feel:

I Look Forward To:

I Am Making Room For This New Habit In My Life By:

Today I Am Asking Myself:

Today I Will Set My Intention On:

The Answer To My Question Above Is:

I Am Maintaining The Positive Habits I Currently Have By:

EVERYDAY I IMAGINE MYSELF WELCOMING IN.....

A NEW WAY OF LIVING

Date: Mood: Days Into New Habit:

The New Habit I Am Forming/Working
On:

I Am Motivated By:

I Plan On Forming This New Habit Today
By:

I Am Noticing:

I Am Letting Go Of The Old Feeling Of:

Despite How I Feel, I WIll:

As I Start Working On My New Habit
Today, I Will Feel:

I Look Forward To:

I Am Making Room For This New Habit In
My Life By:

Today I Am Asking Myself:

Today I Will Set My Intention On:

The Answer To My Question Above Is:

I Am Maintaining The Positive Habits I
Currently Have By:

A NEW WAY OF LIVING

Date: Mood: Days Into New Habit:

The New Habit I Am Forming/Working On:

I Am Motivated By:

I Plan On Forming This New Habit Today By:

I Am Noticing:

I Am Letting Go Of The Old Feeling Of:

Despite How I Feel, I Will:

As I Start Working On My New Habit Today, I Will Feel:

I Look Forward To:

I Am Making Room For This New Habit In My Life By:

Today I Am Asking Myself:

Today I Will Set My Intention On:

The Answer To My Question Above Is:

I Am Maintaining The Positive Habits I Currently Have By:

MY RELEASED THOUGHTS

A NEW WAY OF LIVING

Date: Mood: Days Into New Habit:

The New Habit I Am Forming/Working On: I Am Motivated By:

I Plan On Forming This New Habit Today By: I Am Noticing:

I Am Letting Go Of The Old Feeling Of: Despite How I Feel, I Will:

As I Start Working On My New Habit Today, I Will Feel: I Look Forward To:

I Am Making Room For This New Habit In My Life By: Today I Am Asking Myself:

Today I Will Set My Intention On: The Answer To My Question Above Is:

I Am Maintaining The Positive Habits I Currently Have By:

A NEW WAY OF LIVING

Date: Mood: Days Into New Habit:

The New Habit I Am Forming/Working
On:

I Am Motivated By:

I Plan On Forming This New Habit Today
By:

I Am Noticing:

I Am Letting Go Of The Old Feeling Of:

Despite How I Feel, I Will:

As I Start Working On My New Habit
Today, I Will Feel:

I Look Forward To:

I Am Making Room For This New Habit In
My Life By:

Today I Am Asking Myself:

Today I Will Set My Intention On:

The Answer To My Question Above Is:

I Am Maintaining The Positive Habits I
Currently Have By:

THOUGHT BY THOUGHT AND STEP BY STEP I WILL ACHIEVE.

A NEW WAY OF LIVING

Date: Mood: Days Into New Habit:

The New Habit I Am Forming/Working On:

I Am Motivated By:

I Plan On Forming This New Habit Today By:

I Am Noticing:

I Am Letting Go Of The Old Feeling Of:

Despite How I Feel, I Will:

As I Start Working On My New Habit Today, I Will Feel:

I Look Forward To:

I Am Making Room For This New Habit In My Life By:

Today I Am Asking Myself:

Today I Will Set My Intention On:

The Answer To My Question Above Is:

I Am Maintaining The Positive Habits I Currently Have By:

A NEW WAY OF LIVING

Date: Mood: Days Into New Habit:

The New Habit I Am Forming/Working On:

I Am Motivated By:

I Plan On Forming This New Habit Today By:

I Am Noticing:

I Am Letting Go Of The Old Feeling Of:

Despite How I Feel, I Will:

As I Start Working On My New Habit Today, I Will Feel:

I Look Forward To:

I Am Making Room For This New Habit In My Life By:

Today I Am Asking Myself:

Today I Will Set My Intention On:

The Answer To My Question Above Is:

I Am Maintaining The Positive Habits I Currently Have By:

I MADE UP MY MIND THAT I WILL GET WHAT I WANT.

WHEN I VISUALIZE MYSELF PRACTICING MY NEW HABIT, I ....

A NEW WAY OF LIVING

Date: Mood: Days Into New Habit:

The New Habit I Am Forming/Working
On:

I Am Motivated By:

I Plan On Forming This New Habit Today
By:

I Am Noticing:

I Am Letting Go Of The Old Feeling Of:

Despite How I Feel, I Will:

As I Start Working On My New Habit
Today, I Will Feel:

I Look Forward To:

I Am Making Room For This New Habit In
My Life By:

Today I Am Asking Myself:

Today I Will Set My Intention On:

The Answer To My Question Above Is:

I Am Maintaining The Positive Habits I
Currently Have By:

A NEW WAY OF LIVING

Date: Mood: Days Into New Habit:

The New Habit I Am Forming/Working   I Am Motivated By:
On:

I Plan On Forming This New Habit Today   I Am Noticing:
By:

I Am Letting Go Of The Old Feeling Of: Despite How I Feel, I Will:

As I Start Working On My New Habit   I Look Forward To:
Today, I Will Feel:

I Am Making Room For This New Habit In   Today I Am Asking Myself:
My Life By:

Today I Will Set My Intention On: The Answer To My Question Above Is:

I Am Maintaining The Positive Habits I
Currently Have By:

A NEW WAY OF LIVING

Date: Mood: Days Into New Habit:

The New Habit I Am Forming/Working On:

I Am Motivated By:

I Plan On Forming This New Habit Today By:

I Am Noticing:

I Am Letting Go Of The Old Feeling Of:

Despite How I Feel, I Will:

As I Start Working On My New Habit Today, I Will Feel:

I Look Forward To:

I Am Making Room For This New Habit In My Life By:

Today I Am Asking Myself:

Today I Will Set My Intention On:

The Answer To My Question Above Is:

I Am Maintaining The Positive Habits I Currently Have By:

A NEW WAY OF LIVING

Date: Mood: Days Into New Habit:

The New Habit I Am Forming/Working On:

I Am Motivated By:

I Plan On Forming This New Habit Today By:

I Am Noticing:

I Am Letting Go Of The Old Feeling Of:

Despite How I Feel, I Will:

As I Start Working On My New Habit Today, I Will Feel:

I Look Forward To:

I Am Making Room For This New Habit In My Life By:

Today I Am Asking Myself:

Today I Will Set My Intention On:

The Answer To My Question Above Is:

I Am Maintaining The Positive Habits I Currently Have By:

MY RELEASED THOUGHTS

A NEW WAY OF LIVING

Date: Mood: Days Into New Habit:

The New Habit I Am Forming/Working On: | I Am Motivated By:

I Plan On Forming This New Habit Today By: | I Am Noticing:

I Am Letting Go Of The Old Feeling Of: | Despite How I Feel, I Will:

As I Start Working On My New Habit Today, I Will Feel: | I Look Forward To:

I Am Making Room For This New Habit In My Life By: | Today I Am Asking Myself:

Today I Will Set My Intention On: | The Answer To My Question Above Is:

I Am Maintaining The Positive Habits I Currently Have By:

MY
HAPPINESS
IS A
CULTIVATED
HABIT.

A NEW WAY OF LIVING

Date: Mood: Days Into New Habit:

The New Habit I Am Forming/Working
On:

I Am Motivated By:

I Plan On Forming This New Habit Today
By:

I Am Noticing:

I Am Letting Go Of The Old Feeling Of:

Despite How I Feel, I Will:

As I Start Working On My New Habit
Today, I Will Feel:

I Look Forward To:

I Am Making Room For This New Habit In
My Life By:

Today I Am Asking Myself:

Today I Will Set My Intention On:

The Answer To My Question Above Is:

I Am Maintaining The Positive Habits I
Currently Have By:

A NEW WAY OF LIVING

Date: Mood: Days Into New Habit:

The New Habit I Am Forming/Working On:

I Am Motivated By:

I Plan On Forming This New Habit Today By:

I Am Noticing:

I Am Letting Go Of The Old Feeling Of:

Despite How I Feel, I Will:

As I Start Working On My New Habit Today, I Will Feel:

I Look Forward To:

I Am Making Room For This New Habit In My Life By:

Today I Am Asking Myself:

Today I Will Set My Intention On:

The Answer To My Question Above Is:

I Am Maintaining The Positive Habits I Currently Have By:

A NEW WAY OF LIVING

Date: Mood: Days Into New Habit:

The New Habit I Am Forming/Working On:

I Am Motivated By:

I Plan On Forming This New Habit Today By:

I Am Noticing:

I Am Letting Go Of The Old Feeling Of:

Despite How I Feel, I Will:

As I Start Working On My New Habit Today, I Will Feel:

I Look Forward To:

I Am Making Room For This New Habit In My Life By:

Today I Am Asking Myself:

Today I Will Set My Intention On:

The Answer To My Question Above Is:

I Am Maintaining The Positive Habits I Currently Have By:

I AM THE SOLUTION.

A NEW WAY OF LIVING

Date: Mood: Days Into New Habit:

The New Habit I Am Forming/Working On:

I Am Motivated By:

I Plan On Forming This New Habit Today By:

I Am Noticing:

I Am Letting Go Of The Old Feeling Of:

Despite How I Feel, I Will:

As I Start Working On My New Habit Today, I Will Feel:

I Look Forward To:

I Am Making Room For This New Habit In My Life By:

Today I Am Asking Myself:

Today I Will Set My Intention On:

The Answer To My Question Above Is:

I Am Maintaining The Positive Habits I Currently Have By:

A NEW WAY OF LIVING

Date: Mood: Days Into New Habit:

The New Habit I Am Forming/Working On: | I Am Motivated By:

I Plan On Forming This New Habit Today By: | I Am Noticing:

I Am Letting Go Of The Old Feeling Of: | Despite How I Feel, I Will:

As I Start Working On My New Habit Today, I Will Feel: | I Look Forward To:

I Am Making Room For This New Habit In My Life By: | Today I Am Asking Myself:

Today I Will Set My Intention On: | The Answer To My Question Above Is:

I Am Maintaining The Positive Habits I Currently Have By:

A NEW WAY OF LIVING

Date: Mood: Days Into New Habit:

The New Habit I Am Forming/Working On: I Am Motivated By:

I Plan On Forming This New Habit Today By: I Am Noticing:

I Am Letting Go Of The Old Feeling Of: Despite How I Feel, I Will:

As I Start Working On My New Habit Today, I Will Feel: I Look Forward To:

I Am Making Room For This New Habit In My Life By: Today I Am Asking Myself:

Today I Will Set My Intention On: The Answer To My Question Above Is:

I Am Maintaining The Positive Habits I Currently Have By:

A NEW WAY OF LIVING

Date: Mood: Days Into New Habit:

The New Habit I Am Forming/Working On: | I Am Motivated By:

I Plan On Forming This New Habit Today By: | I Am Noticing:

I Am Letting Go Of The Old Feeling Of: | Despite How I Feel, I Will:

As I Start Working On My New Habit Today, I Will Feel: | I Look Forward To:

I Am Making Room For This New Habit In My Life By: | Today I Am Asking Myself:

Today I Will Set My Intention On: | The Answer To My Question Above Is:

I Am Maintaining The Positive Habits I Currently Have By:

ONCE
I MADE THE DECISION TO CHANGE, EVERYTHING CHANGED.

MY RELEASED THOUGHTS

A NEW WAY OF LIVING

Date: Mood: Days Into New Habit:

The New Habit I Am Forming/Working On: | I Am Motivated By:

I Plan On Forming This New Habit Today By: | I Am Noticing:

I Am Letting Go Of The Old Feeling Of: | Despite How I Feel, I Will:

As I Start Working On My New Habit Today, I Will Feel: | I Look Forward To:

I Am Making Room For This New Habit In My Life By: | Today I Am Asking Myself:

Today I Will Set My Intention On: | The Answer To My Question Above Is:

I Am Maintaining The Positive Habits I Currently Have By:

A NEW WAY OF LIVING

Date: Mood: Days Into New Habit:

The New Habit I Am Forming/Working On:

I Am Motivated By:

I Plan On Forming This New Habit Today By:

I Am Noticing:

I Am Letting Go Of The Old Feeling Of:

Despite How I Feel, I Will:

As I Start Working On My New Habit Today, I Will Feel:

I Look Forward To:

I Am Making Room For This New Habit In My Life By:

Today I Am Asking Myself:

Today I Will Set My Intention On:

The Answer To My Question Above Is:

I Am Maintaining The Positive Habits I Currently Have By:

A NEW WAY OF LIVING

Date: Mood: Days Into New Habit:

The New Habit I Am Forming/Working On:

I Am Motivated By:

I Plan On Forming This New Habit Today By:

I Am Noticing:

I Am Letting Go Of The Old Feeling Of:

Despite How I Feel, I Will:

As I Start Working On My New Habit Today, I Will Feel:

I Look Forward To:

I Am Making Room For This New Habit In My Life By:

Today I Am Asking Myself:

Today I Will Set My Intention On:

The Answer To My Question Above Is:

I Am Maintaining The Positive Habits I Currently Have By:

MY RELEASED THOUGHTS

A NEW WAY OF LIVING

Date: Mood: Days Into New Habit:

The New Habit I Am Forming/Working   I Am Motivated By:
On:

I Plan On Forming This New Habit Today   I Am Noticing:
By:

I Am Letting Go Of The Old Feeling Of: Despite How I Feel, I Will:

As I Start Working On My New Habit   I Look Forward To:
Today, I Will Feel:

I Am Making Room For This New Habit In   Today I Am Asking Myself:
My Life By:

Today I Will Set My Intention On: The Answer To My Question Above Is:

I Am Maintaining The Positive Habits I
Currently Have By:

I AM FULLY COMMITED TO.....

I AM
ALWAYS
IN THE
MOOD
TO BE BETTER
THAN I WAS
YESTERDAY.

A NEW WAY OF LIVING

Date: Mood: Days Into New Habit:

The New Habit I Am Forming/Working On: | I Am Motivated By:

I Plan On Forming This New Habit Today By: | I Am Noticing:

I Am Letting Go Of The Old Feeling Of: | Despite How I Feel, I Will:

As I Start Working On My New Habit Today, I Will Feel: | I Look Forward To:

I Am Making Room For This New Habit In My Life By: | Today I Am Asking Myself:

Today I Will Set My Intention On: | The Answer To My Question Above Is:

I Am Maintaining The Positive Habits I Currently Have By:

A NEW WAY OF LIVING

Date: Mood: Days Into New Habit:

The New Habit I Am Forming/Working On:

I Am Motivated By:

I Plan On Forming This New Habit Today By:

I Am Noticing:

I Am Letting Go Of The Old Feeling Of:

Despite How I Feel, I Will:

As I Start Working On My New Habit Today, I Will Feel:

I Look Forward To:

I Am Making Room For This New Habit In My Life By:

Today I Am Asking Myself:

Today I Will Set My Intention On:

The Answer To My Question Above Is:

I Am Maintaining The Positive Habits I Currently Have By:

A NEW WAY OF LIVING

Date: Mood: Days Into New Habit:

The New Habit I Am Forming/Working On:

I Am Motivated By:

I Plan On Forming This New Habit Today By:

I Am Noticing:

I Am Letting Go Of The Old Feeling Of:

Despite How I Feel, I Will:

As I Start Working On My New Habit Today, I Will Feel:

I Look Forward To:

I Am Making Room For This New Habit In My Life By:

Today I Am Asking Myself:

Today I Will Set My Intention On:

The Answer To My Question Above Is:

I Am Maintaining The Positive Habits I Currently Have By:

MY MOTIVATIONAL MUSIC PLAYLIST CONSIST OF.....

A NEW WAY OF LIVING

Date: Mood: Days Into New Habit:

The New Habit I Am Forming/Working On: | I Am Motivated By:

I Plan On Forming This New Habit Today By: | I Am Noticing:

I Am Letting Go Of The Old Feeling Of: | Despite How I Feel, I Will:

As I Start Working On My New Habit Today, I Will Feel: | I Look Forward To:

I Am Making Room For This New Habit In My Life By: | Today I Am Asking Myself:

Today I Will Set My Intention On: | The Answer To My Question Above Is:

I Am Maintaining The Positive Habits I Currently Have By:

A NEW WAY OF LIVING

Date: Mood: Days Into New Habit:

The New Habit I Am Forming/Working
On:

I Am Motivated By:

I Plan On Forming This New Habit Today
By:

I Am Noticing:

I Am Letting Go Of The Old Feeling Of:

Despite How I Feel, I Will:

As I Start Working On My New Habit
Today, I Will Feel:

I Look Forward To:

I Am Making Room For This New Habit In
My Life By:

Today I Am Asking Myself:

Today I Will Set My Intention On:

The Answer To My Question Above Is:

I Am Maintaining The Positive Habits I
Currently Have By:

A NEW WAY OF LIVING

Date: Mood: Days Into New Habit:

The New Habit I Am Forming/Working On:

I Am Motivated By:

I Plan On Forming This New Habit Today By:

I Am Noticing:

I Am Letting Go Of The Old Feeling Of:

Despite How I Feel, I Will:

As I Start Working On My New Habit Today, I Will Feel:

I Look Forward To:

I Am Making Room For This New Habit In My Life By:

Today I Am Asking Myself:

Today I Will Set My Intention On:

The Answer To My Question Above Is:

I Am Maintaining The Positive Habits I Currently Have By:

I HAVE A
TENDENCY TO....

A NEW WAY OF LIVING

Date: Mood: Days Into New Habit:

The New Habit I Am Forming/Working On:

I Am Motivated By:

I Plan On Forming This New Habit Today By:

I Am Noticing:

I Am Letting Go Of The Old Feeling Of:

Despite How I Feel, I Will:

As I Start Working On My New Habit Today, I Will Feel:

I Look Forward To:

I Am Making Room For This New Habit In My Life By:

Today I Am Asking Myself:

Today I Will Set My Intention On:

The Answer To My Question Above Is:

I Am Maintaining The Positive Habits I Currently Have By:

A NEW WAY OF LIVING

Date: Mood: Days Into New Habit:

The New Habit I Am Forming/Working On: | I Am Motivated By:

I Plan On Forming This New Habit Today By: | I Am Noticing:

I Am Letting Go Of The Old Feeling Of: | Despite How I Feel, I Will:

As I Start Working On My New Habit Today, I Will Feel: | I Look Forward To:

I Am Making Room For This New Habit In My Life By: | Today I Am Asking Myself:

Today I Will Set My Intention On: | The Answer To My Question Above Is:

I Am Maintaining The Positive Habits I Currently Have By:

THE RESULTS KEEP ME GOING.

A NEW WAY OF LIVING

Date: Mood: Days Into New Habit:

The New Habit I Am Forming/Working
On:

I Am Motivated By:

I Plan On Forming This New Habit Today
By:

I Am Noticing:

I Am Letting Go Of The Old Feeling Of:

Despite How I Feel, I Will:

As I Start Working On My New Habit
Today, I Will Feel:

I Look Forward To:

I Am Making Room For This New Habit In
My Life By:

Today I Am Asking Myself:

Today I Will Set My Intention On:

The Answer To My Question Above Is:

I Am Maintaining The Positive Habits I
Currently Have By:

A NEW WAY OF LIVING

Date: Mood: Days Into New Habit:

The New Habit I Am Forming/Working On:

I Am Motivated By:

I Plan On Forming This New Habit Today By:

I Am Noticing:

I Am Letting Go Of The Old Feeling Of:

Despite How I Feel, I Will:

As I Start Working On My New Habit Today, I Will Feel:

I Look Forward To:

I Am Making Room For This New Habit In My Life By:

Today I Am Asking Myself:

Today I Will Set My Intention On:

The Answer To My Question Above Is:

I Am Maintaining The Positive Habits I Currently Have By:

A NEW WAY OF LIVING

Date: Mood: Days Into New Habit:

The New Habit I Am Forming/Working On:

I Am Motivated By:

I Plan On Forming This New Habit Today By:

I Am Noticing:

I Am Letting Go Of The Old Feeling Of:

Despite How I Feel, I Will:

As I Start Working On My New Habit Today, I Will Feel:

I Look Forward To:

I Am Making Room For This New Habit In My Life By:

Today I Am Asking Myself:

Today I Will Set My Intention On:

The Answer To My Question Above Is:

I Am Maintaining The Positive Habits I Currently Have By:

WHEN I DON'T FOLLOW THROUGH WITH MY NEW HABIT I .....

MY RELEASED THOUGHTS

A NEW WAY OF LIVING

Date: Mood: Days Into New Habit:

The New Habit I Am Forming/Working On:

I Am Motivated By:

I Plan On Forming This New Habit Today By:

I Am Noticing:

I Am Letting Go Of The Old Feeling Of:

Despite How I Feel, I Will:

As I Start Working On My New Habit Today, I Will Feel:

I Look Forward To:

I Am Making Room For This New Habit In My Life By:

Today I Am Asking Myself:

Today I Will Set My Intention On:

The Answer To My Question Above Is:

I Am Maintaining The Positive Habits I Currently Have By:

A NEW WAY OF LIVING

Date: Mood: Days Into New Habit:

The New Habit I Am Forming/Working On:

I Am Motivated By:

I Plan On Forming This New Habit Today By:

I Am Noticing:

I Am Letting Go Of The Old Feeling Of:

Despite How I Feel, I Will:

As I Start Working On My New Habit Today, I Will Feel:

I Look Forward To:

I Am Making Room For This New Habit In My Life By:

Today I Am Asking Myself:

Today I Will Set My Intention On:

The Answer To My Question Above Is:

I Am Maintaining The Positive Habits I Currently Have By:

A NEW WAY OF LIVING

Date: Mood: Days Into New Habit:

The New Habit I Am Forming/Working On:

I Am Motivated By:

I Plan On Forming This New Habit Today By:

I Am Noticing:

I Am Letting Go Of The Old Feeling Of:

Despite How I Feel, I Will:

As I Start Working On My New Habit Today, I Will Feel:

I Look Forward To:

I Am Making Room For This New Habit In My Life By:

Today I Am Asking Myself:

Today I Will Set My Intention On:

The Answer To My Question Above Is:

I Am Maintaining The Positive Habits I Currently Have By:

WHEN I DO FOLLOW THROUGH WITH MY NEW HABIT I ....

IT DOESN'T MATTER HOW HARD OR HOW LONG I HAVE TO WORK TO REVERSE A LIFETIME OF BAD HABITS. THEY WILL BE REPLACED WITH GREAT HABITS THAT SERVE ME.

A NEW WAY OF LIVING

Date: Mood: Days Into New Habit:

The New Habit I Am Forming/Working On: | I Am Motivated By:

I Plan On Forming This New Habit Today By: | I Am Noticing:

I Am Letting Go Of The Old Feeling Of: | Despite How I Feel, I Will:

As I Start Working On My New Habit Today, I Will Feel: | I Look Forward To:

I Am Making Room For This New Habit In My Life By: | Today I Am Asking Myself:

Today I Will Set My Intention On: | The Answer To My Question Above Is:

I Am Maintaining The Positive Habits I Currently Have By:

A NEW WAY OF LIVING

Date: Mood: Days Into New Habit:

The New Habit I Am Forming/Working On:

I Am Motivated By:

I Plan On Forming This New Habit Today By:

I Am Noticing:

I Am Letting Go Of The Old Feeling Of:

Despite How I Feel, I Will:

As I Start Working On My New Habit Today, I Will Feel:

I Look Forward To:

I Am Making Room For This New Habit In My Life By:

Today I Am Asking Myself:

Today I Will Set My Intention On:

The Answer To My Question Above Is:

I Am Maintaining The Positive Habits I Currently Have By:

A NEW WAY OF LIVING

Date: Mood: Days Into New Habit:

The New Habit I Am Forming/Working On: | I Am Motivated By:

I Plan On Forming This New Habit Today By: | I Am Noticing:

I Am Letting Go Of The Old Feeling Of: | Despite How I Feel, I Will:

As I Start Working On My New Habit Today, I Will Feel: | I Look Forward To:

I Am Making Room For This New Habit In My Life By: | Today I Am Asking Myself:

Today I Will Set My Intention On: | The Answer To My Question Above Is:

I Am Maintaining The Positive Habits I Currently Have By:

MY RELEASED THOUGHTS

A NEW WAY OF LIVING

Date: Mood: Days Into New Habit:

The New Habit I Am Forming/Working
On:

I Am Motivated By:

I Plan On Forming This New Habit Today
By:

I Am Noticing:

I Am Letting Go Of The Old Feeling Of:

Despite How I Feel, I Will:

As I Start Working On My New Habit
Today, I Will Feel:

I Look Forward To:

I Am Making Room For This New Habit In
My Life By:

Today I Am Asking Myself:

Today I Will Set My Intention On:

The Answer To My Question Above Is:

I Am Maintaining The Positive Habits I
Currently Have By:

A NEW WAY OF LIVING

Date: Mood: Days Into New Habit:

The New Habit I Am Forming/Working   I Am Motivated By:
On:

I Plan On Forming This New Habit Today   I Am Noticing:
By:

I Am Letting Go Of The Old Feeling Of: Despite How I Feel, I Will:

As I Start Working On My New Habit   I Look Forward To:
Today, I Will Feel:

I Am Making Room For This New Habit In   Today I Am Asking Myself:
My Life By:

Today I Will Set My Intention On: The Answer To My Question Above Is:

I Am Maintaining The Positive Habits I
Currently Have By:

ONCE I CONQUERED MYSELF, I WAS ABLE TO CONQUER EVERYTHING ELSE.

- SAYS MY FUTURE SELF

I WILL LOVE ON MYSELF THROUGHOUT THIS PROCESS.

A NEW WAY OF LIVING

Date: Mood: Days Into New Habit:

The New Habit I Am Forming/Working On:

I Am Motivated By:

I Plan On Forming This New Habit Today By:

I Am Noticing:

I Am Letting Go Of The Old Feeling Of:

Despite How I Feel, I Will:

As I Start Working On My New Habit Today, I Will Feel:

I Look Forward To:

I Am Making Room For This New Habit In My Life By:

Today I Am Asking Myself:

Today I Will Set My Intention On:

The Answer To My Question Above Is:

I Am Maintaining The Positive Habits I Currently Have By:

A NEW WAY OF LIVING

Date: Mood: Days Into New Habit:

The New Habit I Am Forming/Working
On:

I Am Motivated By:

I Plan On Forming This New Habit Today
By:

I Am Noticing:

I Am Letting Go Of The Old Feeling Of:

Despite How I Feel, I Will:

As I Start Working On My New Habit
Today, I Will Feel:

I Look Forward To:

I Am Making Room For This New Habit In
My Life By:

Today I Am Asking Myself:

Today I Will Set My Intention On:

The Answer To My Question Above Is:

I Am Maintaining The Positive Habits I
Currently Have By:

A NEW WAY OF LIVING

Date: Mood: Days Into New Habit:

The New Habit I Am Forming/Working On:

I Am Motivated By:

I Plan On Forming This New Habit Today By:

I Am Noticing:

I Am Letting Go Of The Old Feeling Of:

Despite How I Feel, I Will:

As I Start Working On My New Habit Today, I Will Feel:

I Look Forward To:

I Am Making Room For This New Habit In My Life By:

Today I Am Asking Myself:

Today I Will Set My Intention On:

The Answer To My Question Above Is:

I Am Maintaining The Positive Habits I Currently Have By:

A NEW WAY OF LIVING

Date: Mood: Days Into New Habit:

The New Habit I Am Forming/Working On:

I Am Motivated By:

I Plan On Forming This New Habit Today By:

I Am Noticing:

I Am Letting Go Of The Old Feeling Of:

Despite How I Feel, I Will:

As I Start Working On My New Habit Today, I Will Feel:

I Look Forward To:

I Am Making Room For This New Habit In My Life By:

Today I Am Asking Myself:

Today I Will Set My Intention On:

The Answer To My Question Above Is:

I Am Maintaining The Positive Habits I Currently Have By:

MY RELEASED THOUGHTS

A NEW WAY OF LIVING

Date: Mood: Days Into New Habit:

The New Habit I Am Forming/Working On: | I Am Motivated By:

I Plan On Forming This New Habit Today By: | I Am Noticing:

I Am Letting Go Of The Old Feeling Of: | Despite How I Feel, I Will:

As I Start Working On My New Habit Today, I Will Feel: | I Look Forward To:

I Am Making Room For This New Habit In My Life By: | Today I Am Asking Myself:

Today I Will Set My Intention On: | The Answer To My Question Above Is:

I Am Maintaining The Positive Habits I Currently Have By:

A NEW WAY OF LIVING

Date: Mood: Days Into New Habit:

The New Habit I Am Forming/Working
On:

I Am Motivated By:

I Plan On Forming This New Habit Today
By:

I Am Noticing:

I Am Letting Go Of The Old Feeling Of:

Despite How I Feel, I Will:

As I Start Working On My New Habit
Today, I Will Feel:

I Look Forward To:

I Am Making Room For This New Habit In
My Life By:

Today I Am Asking Myself:

Today I Will Set My Intention On:

The Answer To My Question Above Is:

I Am Maintaining The Positive Habits I
Currently Have By:

POSITIVE THOUGHTS I HAVE TOWARDS MYSELF.....

A NEW WAY OF LIVING

Date: Mood: Days Into New Habit:

The New Habit I Am Forming/Working On: I Am Motivated By:

I Plan On Forming This New Habit Today By: I Am Noticing:

I Am Letting Go Of The Old Feeling Of: Despite How I Feel, I Will:

As I Start Working On My New Habit Today, I Will Feel: I Look Forward To:

I Am Making Room For This New Habit In My Life By: Today I Am Asking Myself:

Today I Will Set My Intention On: The Answer To My Question Above Is:

I Am Maintaining The Positive Habits I Currently Have By:

A NEW WAY OF LIVING

Date: Mood: Days Into New Habit:

The New Habit I Am Forming/Working On: | I Am Motivated By:

I Plan On Forming This New Habit Today By: | I Am Noticing:

I Am Letting Go Of The Old Feeling Of: | Despite How I Feel, I Will:

As I Start Working On My New Habit Today, I Will Feel: | I Look Forward To:

I Am Making Room For This New Habit In My Life By: | Today I Am Asking Myself:

Today I Will Set My Intention On: | The Answer To My Question Above Is:

I Am Maintaining The Positive Habits I Currently Have By:

A NEW WAY OF LIVING

Date: Mood: Days Into New Habit:

The New Habit I Am Forming/Working On:

I Am Motivated By:

I Plan On Forming This New Habit Today By:

I Am Noticing:

I Am Letting Go Of The Old Feeling Of:

Despite How I Feel, I Will:

As I Start Working On My New Habit Today, I Will Feel:

I Look Forward To:

I Am Making Room For This New Habit In My Life By:

Today I Am Asking Myself:

Today I Will Set My Intention On:

The Answer To My Question Above Is:

I Am Maintaining The Positive Habits I Currently Have By:

A NEW WAY OF LIVING

Date: Mood: Days Into New Habit:

The New Habit I Am Forming/Working On:

I Am Motivated By:

I Plan On Forming This New Habit Today By:

I Am Noticing:

I Am Letting Go Of The Old Feeling Of:

Despite How I Feel, I Will:

As I Start Working On My New Habit Today, I Will Feel:

I Look Forward To:

I Am Making Room For This New Habit In My Life By:

Today I Am Asking Myself:

Today I Will Set My Intention On:

The Answer To My Question Above Is:

I Am Maintaining The Positive Habits I Currently Have By:

MY RELEASED THOUGHTS

A NEW WAY OF LIVING

Date: Mood: Days Into New Habit:

The New Habit I Am Forming/Working On:

I Am Motivated By:

I Plan On Forming This New Habit Today By:

I Am Noticing:

I Am Letting Go Of The Old Feeling Of:

Despite How I Feel, I Will:

As I Start Working On My New Habit Today, I Will Feel:

I Look Forward To:

I Am Making Room For This New Habit In My Life By:

Today I Am Asking Myself:

Today I Will Set My Intention On:

The Answer To My Question Above Is:

I Am Maintaining The Positive Habits I Currently Have By:

A NEW WAY OF LIVING

Date: Mood: Days Into New Habit:

The New Habit I Am Forming/Working On:

I Am Motivated By:

I Plan On Forming This New Habit Today By:

I Am Noticing:

I Am Letting Go Of The Old Feeling Of:

Despite How I Feel, I Will:

As I Start Working On My New Habit Today, I Will Feel:

I Look Forward To:

I Am Making Room For This New Habit In My Life By:

Today I Am Asking Myself:

Today I Will Set My Intention On:

The Answer To My Question Above Is:

I Am Maintaining The Positive Habits I Currently Have By:

A NEW WAY OF LIVING

Date: Mood: Days Into New Habit:

The New Habit I Am Forming/Working On: I Am Motivated By:

I Plan On Forming This New Habit Today By: I Am Noticing:

I Am Letting Go Of The Old Feeling Of: Despite How I Feel, I Will:

As I Start Working On My New Habit Today, I Will Feel: I Look Forward To:

I Am Making Room For This New Habit In My Life By: Today I Am Asking Myself:

Today I Will Set My Intention On: The Answer To My Question Above Is:

I Am Maintaining The Positive Habits I Currently Have By:

A NEW WAY OF LIVING

Date: Mood: Days Into New Habit:

The New Habit I Am Forming/Working On:

I Am Motivated By:

I Plan On Forming This New Habit Today By:

I Am Noticing:

I Am Letting Go Of The Old Feeling Of:

Despite How I Feel, I Will:

As I Start Working On My New Habit Today, I Will Feel:

I Look Forward To:

I Am Making Room For This New Habit In My Life By:

Today I Am Asking Myself:

Today I Will Set My Intention On:

The Answer To My Question Above Is:

I Am Maintaining The Positive Habits I Currently Have By:

THINGS, PEOPLE AND PLACES I HAVE LET GO OF TO SIMPLIFY MY LIFE.....

A NEW WAY OF LIVING

Date: Mood: Days Into New Habit:

The New Habit I Am Forming/Working On:

I Am Motivated By:

I Plan On Forming This New Habit Today By:

I Am Noticing:

I Am Letting Go Of The Old Feeling Of:

Despite How I Feel, I Will:

As I Start Working On My New Habit Today, I Will Feel:

I Look Forward To:

I Am Making Room For This New Habit In My Life By:

Today I Am Asking Myself:

Today I Will Set My Intention On:

The Answer To My Question Above Is:

I Am Maintaining The Positive Habits I Currently Have By:

A NEW WAY OF LIVING

Date: Mood: Days Into New Habit:

The New Habit I Am Forming/Working On: | I Am Motivated By:

I Plan On Forming This New Habit Today By: | I Am Noticing:

I Am Letting Go Of The Old Feeling Of: | Despite How I Feel, I Will:

As I Start Working On My New Habit Today, I Will Feel: | I Look Forward To:

I Am Making Room For This New Habit In My Life By: | Today I Am Asking Myself:

Today I Will Set My Intention On: | The Answer To My Question Above Is:

I Am Maintaining The Positive Habits I Currently Have By:

A NEW WAY OF LIVING

Date: Mood: Days Into New Habit:

The New Habit I Am Forming/Working On:

I Am Motivated By:

I Plan On Forming This New Habit Today By:

I Am Noticing:

I Am Letting Go Of The Old Feeling Of:

Despite How I Feel, I Will:

As I Start Working On My New Habit Today, I Will Feel:

I Look Forward To:

I Am Making Room For This New Habit In My Life By:

Today I Am Asking Myself:

Today I Will Set My Intention On:

The Answer To My Question Above Is:

I Am Maintaining The Positive Habits I Currently Have By:

I WOULD RATHER THE CHALLENGE OF DISCIPLINE RATHER THEN THE PAIN OF REGRET.

A NEW WAY OF LIVING

Date: Mood: Days Into New Habit:

The New Habit I Am Forming/Working On:

I Am Motivated By:

I Plan On Forming This New Habit Today By:

I Am Noticing:

I Am Letting Go Of The Old Feeling Of:

Despite How I Feel, I Will:

As I Start Working On My New Habit Today, I Will Feel:

I Look Forward To:

I Am Making Room For This New Habit In My Life By:

Today I Am Asking Myself:

Today I Will Set My Intention On:

The Answer To My Question Above Is:

I Am Maintaining The Positive Habits I Currently Have By:

A NEW WAY OF LIVING

Date: Mood: Days Into New Habit:

The New Habit I Am Forming/Working On:

I Am Motivated By:

I Plan On Forming This New Habit Today By:

I Am Noticing:

I Am Letting Go Of The Old Feeling Of:

Despite How I Feel, I Will:

As I Start Working On My New Habit Today, I Will Feel:

I Look Forward To:

I Am Making Room For This New Habit In My Life By:

Today I Am Asking Myself:

Today I Will Set My Intention On:

The Answer To My Question Above Is:

I Am Maintaining The Positive Habits I Currently Have By:

A NEW WAY OF LIVING

Date: Mood: Days Into New Habit:

The New Habit I Am Forming/Working On: | I Am Motivated By:

I Plan On Forming This New Habit Today By: | I Am Noticing:

I Am Letting Go Of The Old Feeling Of: | Despite How I Feel, I Will:

As I Start Working On My New Habit Today, I Will Feel: | I Look Forward To:

I Am Making Room For This New Habit In My Life By: | Today I Am Asking Myself:

Today I Will Set My Intention On: | The Answer To My Question Above Is:

I Am Maintaining The Positive Habits I Currently Have By:

A NEW WAY OF LIVING

Date: Mood: Days Into New Habit:

The New Habit I Am Forming/Working On:

I Am Motivated By:

I Plan On Forming This New Habit Today By:

I Am Noticing:

I Am Letting Go Of The Old Feeling Of:

Despite How I Feel, I Will:

As I Start Working On My New Habit Today, I Will Feel:

I Look Forward To:

I Am Making Room For This New Habit In My Life By:

Today I Am Asking Myself:

Today I Will Set My Intention On:

The Answer To My Question Above Is:

I Am Maintaining The Positive Habits I Currently Have By:

I KNOW I CAN'T GIVE UP ON MYSELF BECAUSE.....

A NEW WAY OF LIVING

Date: Mood: Days Into New Habit:

The New Habit I Am Forming/Working On:

I Am Motivated By:

I Plan On Forming This New Habit Today By:

I Am Noticing:

I Am Letting Go Of The Old Feeling Of:

Despite How I Feel, I Will:

As I Start Working On My New Habit Today, I Will Feel:

I Look Forward To:

I Am Making Room For This New Habit In My Life By:

Today I Am Asking Myself:

Today I Will Set My Intention On:

The Answer To My Question Above Is:

I Am Maintaining The Positive Habits I Currently Have By:

A NEW WAY OF LIVING

Date: Mood: Days Into New Habit:

The New Habit I Am Forming/Working On:	I Am Motivated By:
I Plan On Forming This New Habit Today By:	I Am Noticing:
I Am Letting Go Of The Old Feeling Of:	Despite How I Feel, I Will:
As I Start Working On My New Habit Today, I Will Feel:	I Look Forward To:
I Am Making Room For This New Habit In My Life By:	Today I Am Asking Myself:
Today I Will Set My Intention On:	The Answer To My Question Above Is:
I Am Maintaining The Positive Habits I Currently Have By:	

A NEW WAY OF LIVING

Date: Mood: Days Into New Habit:

The New Habit I Am Forming/Working On:

I Am Motivated By:

I Plan On Forming This New Habit Today By:

I Am Noticing:

I Am Letting Go Of The Old Feeling Of:

Despite How I Feel, I Will:

As I Start Working On My New Habit Today, I Will Feel:

I Look Forward To:

I Am Making Room For This New Habit In My Life By:

Today I Am Asking Myself:

Today I Will Set My Intention On:

The Answer To My Question Above Is:

I Am Maintaining The Positive Habits I Currently Have By:

MY RELEASED THOUGHTS

A NEW WAY OF LIVING

Date: Mood: Days Into New Habit:

The New Habit I Am Forming/Working On:

I Am Motivated By:

I Plan On Forming This New Habit Today By:

I Am Noticing:

I Am Letting Go Of The Old Feeling Of:

Despite How I Feel, I Will:

As I Start Working On My New Habit Today, I Will Feel:

I Look Forward To:

I Am Making Room For This New Habit In My Life By:

Today I Am Asking Myself:

Today I Will Set My Intention On:

The Answer To My Question Above Is:

I Am Maintaining The Positive Habits I Currently Have By:

A NEW WAY OF LIVING

Date: Mood: Days Into New Habit:

The New Habit I Am Forming/Working On:

I Am Motivated By:

I Plan On Forming This New Habit Today By:

I Am Noticing:

I Am Letting Go Of The Old Feeling Of:

Despite How I Feel, I Will:

As I Start Working On My New Habit Today, I Will Feel:

I Look Forward To:

I Am Making Room For This New Habit In My Life By:

Today I Am Asking Myself:

Today I Will Set My Intention On:

The Answer To My Question Above Is:

I Am Maintaining The Positive Habits I Currently Have By:

I AM INSPIRED BY....

A NEW WAY OF LIVING

Date: Mood: Days Into New Habit:

The New Habit I Am Forming/Working On:

I Am Motivated By:

I Plan On Forming This New Habit Today By:

I Am Noticing:

I Am Letting Go Of The Old Feeling Of:

Despite How I Feel, I Will:

As I Start Working On My New Habit Today, I Will Feel:

I Look Forward To:

I Am Making Room For This New Habit In My Life By:

Today I Am Asking Myself:

Today I Will Set My Intention On:

The Answer To My Question Above Is:

I Am Maintaining The Positive Habits I Currently Have By:

A NEW WAY OF LIVING

Date: Mood: Days Into New Habit:

The New Habit I Am Forming/Working On:

I Am Motivated By:

I Plan On Forming This New Habit Today By:

I Am Noticing:

I Am Letting Go Of The Old Feeling Of:

Despite How I Feel, I Will:

As I Start Working On My New Habit Today, I Will Feel:

I Look Forward To:

I Am Making Room For This New Habit In My Life By:

Today I Am Asking Myself:

Today I Will Set My Intention On:

The Answer To My Question Above Is:

I Am Maintaining The Positive Habits I Currently Have By:

MY RELEASED THOUGHTS

A NEW WAY OF LIVING

Date: Mood: Days Into New Habit:

The New Habit I Am Forming/Working On:

I Am Motivated By:

I Plan On Forming This New Habit Today By:

I Am Noticing:

I Am Letting Go Of The Old Feeling Of:

Despite How I Feel, I Will:

As I Start Working On My New Habit Today, I Will Feel:

I Look Forward To:

I Am Making Room For This New Habit In My Life By:

Today I Am Asking Myself:

Today I Will Set My Intention On:

The Answer To My Question Above Is:

I Am Maintaining The Positive Habits I Currently Have By:

A NEW WAY OF LIVING

Date: _____ Mood: _____ Days Into New Habit: _____

The New Habit I Am Forming/Working On:

I Am Motivated By:

I Plan On Forming This New Habit Today By:

I Am Noticing:

I Am Letting Go Of The Old Feeling Of:

Despite How I Feel, I Will:

As I Start Working On My New Habit Today, I Will Feel:

I Look Forward To:

I Am Making Room For This New Habit In My Life By:

Today I Am Asking Myself:

Today I Will Set My Intention On:

The Answer To My Question Above Is:

I Am Maintaining The Positive Habits I Currently Have By:

ANYTHING IS POSSIBLE BECAUSE I AM FOCUSED AND DISCIPLINED ENOUGH TO GET WHAT I WANT.

I AM SO GRATEFUL FOR.....

A NEW WAY OF LIVING

Date: Mood: Days Into New Habit:

The New Habit I Am Forming/Working On:	I Am Motivated By:
I Plan On Forming This New Habit Today By:	I Am Noticing:
I Am Letting Go Of The Old Feeling Of:	Despite How I Feel, I Will:
As I Start Working On My New Habit Today, I Will Feel:	I Look Forward To:
I Am Making Room For This New Habit In My Life By:	Today I Am Asking Myself:
Today I Will Set My Intention On:	The Answer To My Question Above Is:
I Am Maintaining The Positive Habits I Currently Have By:	

A NEW WAY OF LIVING

Date: Mood: Days Into New Habit:

The New Habit I Am Forming/Working On:

I Am Motivated By:

I Plan On Forming This New Habit Today By:

I Am Noticing:

I Am Letting Go Of The Old Feeling Of:

Despite How I Feel, I Will:

As I Start Working On My New Habit Today, I Will Feel:

I Look Forward To:

I Am Making Room For This New Habit In My Life By:

Today I Am Asking Myself:

Today I Will Set My Intention On:

The Answer To My Question Above Is:

I Am Maintaining The Positive Habits I Currently Have By:

I RESPECT MY EFFORTS AND MY ABILITY TO KEEP GOING.

A NEW WAY OF LIVING

Date: Mood: Days Into New Habit:

The New Habit I Am Forming/Working On:

I Am Motivated By:

I Plan On Forming This New Habit Today By:

I Am Noticing:

I Am Letting Go Of The Old Feeling Of:

Despite How I Feel, I Will:

As I Start Working On My New Habit Today, I Will Feel:

I Look Forward To:

I Am Making Room For This New Habit In My Life By:

Today I Am Asking Myself:

Today I Will Set My Intention On:

The Answer To My Question Above Is:

I Am Maintaining The Positive Habits I Currently Have By:

A NEW WAY OF LIVING

Date: Mood: Days Into New Habit:

The New Habit I Am Forming/Working On: I Am Motivated By:

I Plan On Forming This New Habit Today By: I Am Noticing:

I Am Letting Go Of The Old Feeling Of: Despite How I Feel, I Will:

As I Start Working On My New Habit Today, I Will Feel: I Look Forward To:

I Am Making Room For This New Habit In My Life By: Today I Am Asking Myself:

Today I Will Set My Intention On: The Answer To My Question Above Is:

I Am Maintaining The Positive Habits I Currently Have By:

A NEW WAY OF LIVING

Date: Mood: Days Into New Habit:

The New Habit I Am Forming/Working On:

I Am Motivated By:

I Plan On Forming This New Habit Today By:

I Am Noticing:

I Am Letting Go Of The Old Feeling Of:

Despite How I Feel, I Will:

As I Start Working On My New Habit Today, I Will Feel:

I Look Forward To:

I Am Making Room For This New Habit In My Life By:

Today I Am Asking Myself:

Today I Will Set My Intention On:

The Answer To My Question Above Is:

I Am Maintaining The Positive Habits I Currently Have By:

A NEW WAY OF LIVING

Date: Mood: Days Into New Habit:

The New Habit I Am Forming/Working On:

I Am Motivated By:

I Plan On Forming This New Habit Today By:

I Am Noticing:

I Am Letting Go Of The Old Feeling Of:

Despite How I Feel, I Will:

As I Start Working On My New Habit Today, I Will Feel:

I Look Forward To:

I Am Making Room For This New Habit In My Life By:

Today I Am Asking Myself:

Today I Will Set My Intention On:

The Answer To My Question Above Is:

I Am Maintaining The Positive Habits I Currently Have By:

ACTIVITIES THAT INSPIRE ME.....

MY RELEASED THOUGHTS

A NEW WAY OF LIVING

Date: Mood: Days Into New Habit:

The New Habit I Am Forming/Working On: I Am Motivated By:

I Plan On Forming This New Habit Today By: I Am Noticing:

I Am Letting Go Of The Old Feeling Of: Despite How I Feel, I Will:

As I Start Working On My New Habit Today, I Will Feel: I Look Forward To:

I Am Making Room For This New Habit In My Life By: Today I Am Asking Myself:

Today I Will Set My Intention On: The Answer To My Question Above Is:

I Am Maintaining The Positive Habits I Currently Have By:

A NEW WAY OF LIVING

Date: Mood: Days Into New Habit:

The New Habit I Am Forming/Working On:

I Am Motivated By:

I Plan On Forming This New Habit Today By:

I Am Noticing:

I Am Letting Go Of The Old Feeling Of:

Despite How I Feel, I Will:

As I Start Working On My New Habit Today, I Will Feel:

I Look Forward To:

I Am Making Room For This New Habit In My Life By:

Today I Am Asking Myself:

Today I Will Set My Intention On:

The Answer To My Question Above Is:

I Am Maintaining The Positive Habits I Currently Have By:

A NEW WAY OF LIVING

Date: Mood: Days Into New Habit:

The New Habit I Am Forming/Working On:

I Am Motivated By:

I Plan On Forming This New Habit Today By:

I Am Noticing:

I Am Letting Go Of The Old Feeling Of:

Despite How I Feel, I Will:

As I Start Working On My New Habit Today, I Will Feel:

I Look Forward To:

I Am Making Room For This New Habit In My Life By:

Today I Am Asking Myself:

Today I Will Set My Intention On:

The Answer To My Question Above Is:

I Am Maintaining The Positive Habits I Currently Have By:

A NEW WAY OF LIVING

Date: Mood: Days Into New Habit:

The New Habit I Am Forming/Working On: | I Am Motivated By:

I Plan On Forming This New Habit Today By: | I Am Noticing:

I Am Letting Go Of The Old Feeling Of: | Despite How I Feel, I Will:

As I Start Working On My New Habit Today, I Will Feel: | I Look Forward To:

I Am Making Room For This New Habit In My Life By: | Today I Am Asking Myself:

Today I Will Set My Intention On: | The Answer To My Question Above Is:

I Am Maintaining The Positive Habits I Currently Have By:

A NEW WAY OF LIVING

Date: Mood: Days Into New Habit:

The New Habit I Am Forming/Working   I Am Motivated By:
On:

I Plan On Forming This New Habit Today   I Am Noticing:
By:

I Am Letting Go Of The Old Feeling Of: Despite How I Feel, I Will:

As I Start Working On My New Habit   I Look Forward To:
Today, I Will Feel:

I Am Making Room For This New Habit In   Today I Am Asking Myself:
My Life By:

Today I Will Set My Intention On: The Answer To My Question Above Is:

I Am Maintaining The Positive Habits I
Currently Have By:

50 THINGS MY NEW HABIT WILL HELP ME ACHIEVE....

THESE BELIEFS ARE HOLDING ME BACK.....

A NEW WAY OF LIVING

Date: Mood: Days Into New Habit:

The New Habit I Am Forming/Working On: I Am Motivated By:

I Plan On Forming This New Habit Today By: I Am Noticing:

I Am Letting Go Of The Old Feeling Of: Despite How I Feel, I Will:

As I Start Working On My New Habit Today, I Will Feel: I Look Forward To:

I Am Making Room For This New Habit In My Life By: Today I Am Asking Myself:

Today I Will Set My Intention On: The Answer To My Question Above Is:

I Am Maintaining The Positive Habits I Currently Have By:

A NEW WAY OF LIVING

Date: Mood: Days Into New Habit:

The New Habit I Am Forming/Working   I Am Motivated By:
On:

I Plan On Forming This New Habit Today   I Am Noticing:
By:

I Am Letting Go Of The Old Feeling Of: Despite How I Feel, I Will:

As I Start Working On My New Habit   I Look Forward To:
Today, I Will Feel:

I Am Making Room For This New Habit In   Today I Am Asking Myself:
My Life By:

Today I Will Set My Intention On: The Answer To My Question Above Is:

I Am Maintaining The Positive Habits I
Currently Have By:

A NEW WAY OF LIVING

Date: Mood: Days Into New Habit:

The New Habit I Am Forming/Working On: | I Am Motivated By:

I Plan On Forming This New Habit Today By: | I Am Noticing:

I Am Letting Go Of The Old Feeling Of: | Despite How I Feel, I Will:

As I Start Working On My New Habit Today, I Will Feel: | I Look Forward To:

I Am Making Room For This New Habit In My Life By: | Today I Am Asking Myself:

Today I Will Set My Intention On: | The Answer To My Question Above Is:

I Am Maintaining The Positive Habits I Currently Have By:

A NEW WAY OF LIVING

Date: Mood: Days Into New Habit:

The New Habit I Am Forming/Working On:

I Am Motivated By:

I Plan On Forming This New Habit Today By:

I Am Noticing:

I Am Letting Go Of The Old Feeling Of:

Despite How I Feel, I Will:

As I Start Working On My New Habit Today, I Will Feel:

I Look Forward To:

I Am Making Room For This New Habit In My Life By:

Today I Am Asking Myself:

Today I Will Set My Intention On:

The Answer To My Question Above Is:

I Am Maintaining The Positive Habits I Currently Have By:

I HAVE THE WILL TO ACHIEVE WHAT I WANT.

A NEW WAY OF LIVING

Date: Mood: Days Into New Habit:

The New Habit I Am Forming/Working On: I Am Motivated By:

I Plan On Forming This New Habit Today By: I Am Noticing:

I Am Letting Go Of The Old Feeling Of: Despite How I Feel, I Will:

As I Start Working On My New Habit Today, I Will Feel: I Look Forward To:

I Am Making Room For This New Habit In My Life By: Today I Am Asking Myself:

Today I Will Set My Intention On: The Answer To My Question Above Is:

I Am Maintaining The Positive Habits I Currently Have By:

A NEW WAY OF LIVING

Date: Mood: Days Into New Habit:

The New Habit I Am Forming/Working On:

I Am Motivated By:

I Plan On Forming This New Habit Today By:

I Am Noticing:

I Am Letting Go Of The Old Feeling Of:

Despite How I Feel, I Will:

As I Start Working On My New Habit Today, I Will Feel:

I Look Forward To:

I Am Making Room For This New Habit In My Life By:

Today I Am Asking Myself:

Today I Will Set My Intention On:

The Answer To My Question Above Is:

I Am Maintaining The Positive Habits I Currently Have By:

A NEW WAY OF LIVING

Date: Mood: Days Into New Habit:

The New Habit I Am Forming/Working On: | I Am Motivated By:

I Plan On Forming This New Habit Today By: | I Am Noticing:

I Am Letting Go Of The Old Feeling Of: | Despite How I Feel, I Will:

As I Start Working On My New Habit Today, I Will Feel: | I Look Forward To:

I Am Making Room For This New Habit In My Life By: | Today I Am Asking Myself:

Today I Will Set My Intention On: | The Answer To My Question Above Is:

I Am Maintaining The Positive Habits I Currently Have By:

A NEW WAY OF LIVING

Date: Mood: Days Into New Habit:

The New Habit I Am Forming/Working On:

I Am Motivated By:

I Plan On Forming This New Habit Today By:

I Am Noticing:

I Am Letting Go Of The Old Feeling Of:

Despite How I Feel, I Will:

As I Start Working On My New Habit Today, I Will Feel:

I Look Forward To:

I Am Making Room For This New Habit In My Life By:

Today I Am Asking Myself:

Today I Will Set My Intention On:

The Answer To My Question Above Is:

I Am Maintaining The Positive Habits I Currently Have By:

MY RELEASED THOUGHTS

A NEW WAY OF LIVING

Date: Mood: Days Into New Habit:

The New Habit I Am Forming/Working On:

I Am Motivated By:

I Plan On Forming This New Habit Today By:

I Am Noticing:

I Am Letting Go Of The Old Feeling Of:

Despite How I Feel, I Will:

As I Start Working On My New Habit Today, I Will Feel:

I Look Forward To:

I Am Making Room For This New Habit In My Life By:

Today I Am Asking Myself:

Today I Will Set My Intention On:

The Answer To My Question Above Is:

I Am Maintaining The Positive Habits I Currently Have By:

A NEW WAY OF LIVING

Date: Mood: Days Into New Habit:

The New Habit I Am Forming/Working
On:

I Am Motivated By:

I Plan On Forming This New Habit Today
By:

I Am Noticing:

I Am Letting Go Of The Old Feeling Of:

Despite How I Feel, I Will:

As I Start Working On My New Habit
Today, I Will Feel:

I Look Forward To:

I Am Making Room For This New Habit In
My Life By:

Today I Am Asking Myself:

Today I Will Set My Intention On:

The Answer To My Question Above Is:

I Am Maintaining The Positive Habits I
Currently Have By:

A NEW WAY OF LIVING

Date: Mood: Days Into New Habit:

The New Habit I Am Forming/Working On: I Am Motivated By:

I Plan On Forming This New Habit Today By: I Am Noticing:

I Am Letting Go Of The Old Feeling Of: Despite How I Feel, I Will:

As I Start Working On My New Habit Today, I Will Feel: I Look Forward To:

I Am Making Room For This New Habit In My Life By: Today I Am Asking Myself:

Today I Will Set My Intention On: The Answer To My Question Above Is:

I Am Maintaining The Positive Habits I Currently Have By:

A NEW WAY OF LIVING

Date: Mood: Days Into New Habit:

The New Habit I Am Forming/Working
On:

I Am Motivated By:

I Plan On Forming This New Habit Today
By:

I Am Noticing:

I Am Letting Go Of The Old Feeling Of:

Despite How I Feel, I Will:

As I Start Working On My New Habit
Today, I Will Feel:

I Look Forward To:

I Am Making Room For This New Habit In
My Life By:

Today I Am Asking Myself:

Today I Will Set My Intention On:

The Answer To My Question Above Is:

I Am Maintaining The Positive Habits I
Currently Have By:

I DON'T CREATE EXCUSES. I CREATE RESULTS.

A NEW WAY OF LIVING

Date: Mood: Days Into New Habit:

The New Habit I Am Forming/Working On:

I Am Motivated By:

I Plan On Forming This New Habit Today By:

I Am Noticing:

I Am Letting Go Of The Old Feeling Of:

Despite How I Feel, I Will:

As I Start Working On My New Habit Today, I Will Feel:

I Look Forward To:

I Am Making Room For This New Habit In My Life By:

Today I Am Asking Myself:

Today I Will Set My Intention On:

The Answer To My Question Above Is:

I Am Maintaining The Positive Habits I Currently Have By:

ONCE I MADE THE DECISION TO CHANGE, I STARTED....

MY RELEASED THOUGHTS

A NEW WAY OF LIVING

Date: Mood: Days Into New Habit:

The New Habit I Am Forming/Working On:

I Am Motivated By:

I Plan On Forming This New Habit Today By:

I Am Noticing:

I Am Letting Go Of The Old Feeling Of:

Despite How I Feel, I Will:

As I Start Working On My New Habit Today, I Will Feel:

I Look Forward To:

I Am Making Room For This New Habit In My Life By:

Today I Am Asking Myself:

Today I Will Set My Intention On:

The Answer To My Question Above Is:

I Am Maintaining The Positive Habits I Currently Have By:

A NEW WAY OF LIVING

Date: Mood: Days Into New Habit:

The New Habit I Am Forming/Working On:

I Am Motivated By:

I Plan On Forming This New Habit Today By:

I Am Noticing:

I Am Letting Go Of The Old Feeling Of:

Despite How I Feel, I Will:

As I Start Working On My New Habit Today, I Will Feel:

I Look Forward To:

I Am Making Room For This New Habit In My Life By:

Today I Am Asking Myself:

Today I Will Set My Intention On:

The Answer To My Question Above Is:

I Am Maintaining The Positive Habits I Currently Have By:

A NEW WAY OF LIVING

Date: Mood: Days Into New Habit:

The New Habit I Am Forming/Working On: | I Am Motivated By:

I Plan On Forming This New Habit Today By: | I Am Noticing:

I Am Letting Go Of The Old Feeling Of: | Despite How I Feel, I Will:

As I Start Working On My New Habit Today, I Will Feel: | I Look Forward To:

I Am Making Room For This New Habit In My Life By: | Today I Am Asking Myself:

Today I Will Set My Intention On: | The Answer To My Question Above Is:

I Am Maintaining The Positive Habits I Currently Have By:

MY RELEASED THOUGHTS

A NEW WAY OF LIVING

Date: Mood: Days Into New Habit:

The New Habit I Am Forming/Working On:

I Am Motivated By:

I Plan On Forming This New Habit Today By:

I Am Noticing:

I Am Letting Go Of The Old Feeling Of:

Despite How I Feel, I Will:

As I Start Working On My New Habit Today, I Will Feel:

I Look Forward To:

I Am Making Room For This New Habit In My Life By:

Today I Am Asking Myself:

Today I Will Set My Intention On:

The Answer To My Question Above Is:

I Am Maintaining The Positive Habits I Currently Have By:

187

A NEW WAY OF LIVING

Date: Mood: Days Into New Habit:

The New Habit I Am Forming/Working On: | I Am Motivated By:

I Plan On Forming This New Habit Today By: | I Am Noticing:

I Am Letting Go Of The Old Feeling Of: | Despite How I Feel, I Will:

As I Start Working On My New Habit Today, I Will Feel: | I Look Forward To:

I Am Making Room For This New Habit In My Life By: | Today I Am Asking Myself:

Today I Will Set My Intention On: | The Answer To My Question Above Is:

I Am Maintaining The Positive Habits I Currently Have By:

I MANAGE STRESS BY.....

A NEW WAY OF LIVING

Date: Mood: Days Into New Habit:

The New Habit I Am Forming/Working
On:

I Am Motivated By:

I Plan On Forming This New Habit Today
By:

I Am Noticing:

I Am Letting Go Of The Old Feeling Of:

Despite How I Feel, I Will:

As I Start Working On My New Habit
Today, I Will Feel:

I Look Forward To:

I Am Making Room For This New Habit In
My Life By:

Today I Am Asking Myself:

Today I Will Set My Intention On:

The Answer To My Question Above Is:

I Am Maintaining The Positive Habits I
Currently Have By:

A NEW WAY OF LIVING

Date: Mood: Days Into New Habit:

The New Habit I Am Forming/Working On:

I Am Motivated By:

I Plan On Forming This New Habit Today By:

I Am Noticing:

I Am Letting Go Of The Old Feeling Of:

Despite How I Feel, I Will:

As I Start Working On My New Habit Today, I Will Feel:

I Look Forward To:

I Am Making Room For This New Habit In My Life By:

Today I Am Asking Myself:

Today I Will Set My Intention On:

The Answer To My Question Above Is:

I Am Maintaining The Positive Habits I Currently Have By:

MY RELEASED THOUGHTS

A NEW WAY OF LIVING

Date: Mood: Days Into New Habit:

The New Habit I Am Forming/Working On:

I Am Motivated By:

I Plan On Forming This New Habit Today By:

I Am Noticing:

I Am Letting Go Of The Old Feeling Of:

Despite How I Feel, I Will:

As I Start Working On My New Habit Today, I Will Feel:

I Look Forward To:

I Am Making Room For This New Habit In My Life By:

Today I Am Asking Myself:

Today I Will Set My Intention On:

The Answer To My Question Above Is:

I Am Maintaining The Positive Habits I Currently Have By:

A NEW WAY OF LIVING

Date: Mood: Days Into New Habit:

The New Habit I Am Forming/Working On:

I Am Motivated By:

I Plan On Forming This New Habit Today By:

I Am Noticing:

I Am Letting Go Of The Old Feeling Of:

Despite How I Feel, I Will:

As I Start Working On My New Habit Today, I Will Feel:

I Look Forward To:

I Am Making Room For This New Habit In My Life By:

Today I Am Asking Myself:

Today I Will Set My Intention On:

The Answer To My Question Above Is:

I Am Maintaining The Positive Habits I Currently Have By:

RIGHT NOW I AM FEELING....

A NEW WAY OF LIVING

Date: Mood: Days Into New Habit:

The New Habit I Am Forming/Working On:	I Am Motivated By:
I Plan On Forming This New Habit Today By:	I Am Noticing:
I Am Letting Go Of The Old Feeling Of:	Despite How I Feel, I Will:
As I Start Working On My New Habit Today, I Will Feel:	I Look Forward To:
I Am Making Room For This New Habit In My Life By:	Today I Am Asking Myself:
Today I Will Set My Intention On:	The Answer To My Question Above Is:
I Am Maintaining The Positive Habits I Currently Have By:	

A NEW WAY OF LIVING

Date: Mood: Days Into New Habit:

The New Habit I Am Forming/Working On:

I Am Motivated By:

I Plan On Forming This New Habit Today By:

I Am Noticing:

I Am Letting Go Of The Old Feeling Of:

Despite How I Feel, I Will:

As I Start Working On My New Habit Today, I Will Feel:

I Look Forward To:

I Am Making Room For This New Habit In My Life By:

Today I Am Asking Myself:

Today I Will Set My Intention On:

The Answer To My Question Above Is:

I Am Maintaining The Positive Habits I Currently Have By:

MY RELEASED THOUGHTS

A NEW WAY OF LIVING

Date: Mood: Days Into New Habit:

The New Habit I Am Forming/Working On:

I Am Motivated By:

I Plan On Forming This New Habit Today By:

I Am Noticing:

I Am Letting Go Of The Old Feeling Of:

Despite How I Feel, I Will:

As I Start Working On My New Habit Today, I Will Feel:

I Look Forward To:

I Am Making Room For This New Habit In My Life By:

Today I Am Asking Myself:

Today I Will Set My Intention On:

The Answer To My Question Above Is:

I Am Maintaining The Positive Habits I Currently Have By:

A NEW WAY OF LIVING

Date: Mood: Days Into New Habit:

The New Habit I Am Forming/Working   I Am Motivated By:
On:

I Plan On Forming This New Habit Today   I Am Noticing:
By:

I Am Letting Go Of The Old Feeling Of: Despite How I Feel, I Will:

As I Start Working On My New Habit   I Look Forward To:
Today, I Will Feel:

I Am Making Room For This New Habit In   Today I Am Asking Myself:
My Life By:

Today I Will Set My Intention On: The Answer To My Question Above Is:

I Am Maintaining The Positive Habits I
Currently Have By:

A NEW WAY OF LIVING

Date: Mood: Days Into New Habit:

The New Habit I Am Forming/Working On: | I Am Motivated By:

I Plan On Forming This New Habit Today By: | I Am Noticing:

I Am Letting Go Of The Old Feeling Of: | Despite How I Feel, I Will:

As I Start Working On My New Habit Today, I Will Feel: | I Look Forward To:

I Am Making Room For This New Habit In My Life By: | Today I Am Asking Myself:

Today I Will Set My Intention On: | The Answer To My Question Above Is:

I Am Maintaining The Positive Habits I Currently Have By:

A NEW WAY OF LIVING

Date: Mood: Days Into New Habit:

The New Habit I Am Forming/Working On:

I Am Motivated By:

I Plan On Forming This New Habit Today By:

I Am Noticing:

I Am Letting Go Of The Old Feeling Of:

Despite How I Feel, I Will:

As I Start Working On My New Habit Today, I Will Feel:

I Look Forward To:

I Am Making Room For This New Habit In My Life By:

Today I Am Asking Myself:

Today I Will Set My Intention On:

The Answer To My Question Above Is:

I Am Maintaining The Positive Habits I Currently Have By:

I DO WHAT NEEDS TO BE DONE EVEN WHEN I DON'T WANT TO DO IT. IT'S WHAT YOU DO WHEN YOU ARE READY TO ACHIEVE.

I CAN DO ANYTHING I PUT MY MIND TO.

A NEW WAY OF LIVING

Date: Mood: Days Into New Habit:

The New Habit I Am Forming/Working On:

I Am Motivated By:

I Plan On Forming This New Habit Today By:

I Am Noticing:

I Am Letting Go Of The Old Feeling Of:

Despite How I Feel, I Will:

As I Start Working On My New Habit Today, I Will Feel:

I Look Forward To:

I Am Making Room For This New Habit In My Life By:

Today I Am Asking Myself:

Today I Will Set My Intention On:

The Answer To My Question Above Is:

I Am Maintaining The Positive Habits I Currently Have By:

A NEW WAY OF LIVING

Date: Mood: Days Into New Habit:

The New Habit I Am Forming/Working On:

I Am Motivated By:

I Plan On Forming This New Habit Today By:

I Am Noticing:

I Am Letting Go Of The Old Feeling Of:

Despite How I Feel, I Will:

As I Start Working On My New Habit Today, I Will Feel:

I Look Forward To:

I Am Making Room For This New Habit In My Life By:

Today I Am Asking Myself:

Today I Will Set My Intention On:

The Answer To My Question Above Is:

I Am Maintaining The Positive Habits I Currently Have By:

MY RELEASED THOUGHTS

A NEW WAY OF LIVING

Date: Mood: Days Into New Habit:

The New Habit I Am Forming/Working   I Am Motivated By:
On:

I Plan On Forming This New Habit Today   I Am Noticing:
By:

I Am Letting Go Of The Old Feeling Of: Despite How I Feel, I Will:

As I Start Working On My New Habit   I Look Forward To:
Today, I Will Feel:

I Am Making Room For This New Habit In   Today I Am Asking Myself:
My Life By:

Today I Will Set My Intention On: The Answer To My Question Above Is:

I Am Maintaining The Positive Habits I
Currently Have By:

A NEW WAY OF LIVING

Date: Mood: Days Into New Habit:

The New Habit I Am Forming/Working On:

I Am Motivated By:

I Plan On Forming This New Habit Today By:

I Am Noticing:

I Am Letting Go Of The Old Feeling Of:

Despite How I Feel, I Will:

As I Start Working On My New Habit Today, I Will Feel:

I Look Forward To:

I Am Making Room For This New Habit In My Life By:

Today I Am Asking Myself:

Today I Will Set My Intention On:

The Answer To My Question Above Is:

I Am Maintaining The Positive Habits I Currently Have By:

A NEW WAY OF LIVING

Date: Mood: Days Into New Habit:

The New Habit I Am Forming/Working On:

I Am Motivated By:

I Plan On Forming This New Habit Today By:

I Am Noticing:

I Am Letting Go Of The Old Feeling Of:

Despite How I Feel, I Will:

As I Start Working On My New Habit Today, I Will Feel:

I Look Forward To:

I Am Making Room For This New Habit In My Life By:

Today I Am Asking Myself:

Today I Will Set My Intention On:

The Answer To My Question Above Is:

I Am Maintaining The Positive Habits I Currently Have By:

A FEW THINGS I HOLD CLOSE TO MY HEART ARE.....

I UNPLUG BY.....

A NEW WAY OF LIVING

Date: Mood: Days Into New Habit:

The New Habit I Am Forming/Working On:

I Am Motivated By:

I Plan On Forming This New Habit Today By:

I Am Noticing:

I Am Letting Go Of The Old Feeling Of:

Despite How I Feel, I Will:

As I Start Working On My New Habit Today, I Will Feel:

I Look Forward To:

I Am Making Room For This New Habit In My Life By:

Today I Am Asking Myself:

Today I Will Set My Intention On:

The Answer To My Question Above Is:

I Am Maintaining The Positive Habits I Currently Have By:

A NEW WAY OF LIVING

Date: Mood: Days Into New Habit:

The New Habit I Am Forming/Working On:

I Am Motivated By:

I Plan On Forming This New Habit Today By:

I Am Noticing:

I Am Letting Go Of The Old Feeling Of:

Despite How I Feel, I Will:

As I Start Working On My New Habit Today, I Will Feel:

I Look Forward To:

I Am Making Room For This New Habit In My Life By:

Today I Am Asking Myself:

Today I Will Set My Intention On:

The Answer To My Question Above Is:

I Am Maintaining The Positive Habits I Currently Have By:

A NEW WAY OF LIVING

Date: Mood: Days Into New Habit:

The New Habit I Am Forming/Working On:

I Am Motivated By:

I Plan On Forming This New Habit Today By:

I Am Noticing:

I Am Letting Go Of The Old Feeling Of:

Despite How I Feel, I Will:

As I Start Working On My New Habit Today, I Will Feel:

I Look Forward To:

I Am Making Room For This New Habit In My Life By:

Today I Am Asking Myself:

Today I Will Set My Intention On:

The Answer To My Question Above Is:

I Am Maintaining The Positive Habits I Currently Have By:

A NEW WAY OF LIVING

Date: Mood: Days Into New Habit:

The New Habit I Am Forming/Working On:	I Am Motivated By:
I Plan On Forming This New Habit Today By:	I Am Noticing:
I Am Letting Go Of The Old Feeling Of:	Despite How I Feel, I Will:
As I Start Working On My New Habit Today, I Will Feel:	I Look Forward To:
I Am Making Room For This New Habit In My Life By:	Today I Am Asking Myself:
Today I Will Set My Intention On:	The Answer To My Question Above Is:
I Am Maintaining The Positive Habits I Currently Have By:	

MY RELEASED THOUGHTS

I WILL GET IT DONE WITH OR WITHOUT SUPPORT.

A NEW WAY OF LIVING

Date: Mood: Days Into New Habit:

The New Habit I Am Forming/Working On:

I Am Motivated By:

I Plan On Forming This New Habit Today By:

I Am Noticing:

I Am Letting Go Of The Old Feeling Of:

Despite How I Feel, I Will:

As I Start Working On My New Habit Today, I Will Feel:

I Look Forward To:

I Am Making Room For This New Habit In My Life By:

Today I Am Asking Myself:

Today I Will Set My Intention On:

The Answer To My Question Above Is:

I Am Maintaining The Positive Habits I Currently Have By:

A NEW WAY OF LIVING

Date: Mood: Days Into New Habit:

The New Habit I Am Forming/Working On: I Am Motivated By:

I Plan On Forming This New Habit Today By: I Am Noticing:

I Am Letting Go Of The Old Feeling Of: Despite How I Feel, I Will:

As I Start Working On My New Habit Today, I Will Feel: I Look Forward To:

I Am Making Room For This New Habit In My Life By: Today I Am Asking Myself:

Today I Will Set My Intention On: The Answer To My Question Above Is:

I Am Maintaining The Positive Habits I Currently Have By:

SOME SMALL ACTIONS THAT I AM TAKING THAT WILL MAKE A POSITIVE DIFFERENCE ARE.....

#MINDFULNESS

A NEW WAY OF LIVING

Date: Mood: Days Into New Habit:

The New Habit I Am Forming/Working On:

I Am Motivated By:

I Plan On Forming This New Habit Today By:

I Am Noticing:

I Am Letting Go Of The Old Feeling Of:

Despite How I Feel, I Will:

As I Start Working On My New Habit Today, I Will Feel:

I Look Forward To:

I Am Making Room For This New Habit In My Life By:

Today I Am Asking Myself:

Today I Will Set My Intention On:

The Answer To My Question Above Is:

I Am Maintaining The Positive Habits I Currently Have By:

MY RELEASED THOUGHTS

A NEW WAY OF LIVING

Date: Mood: Days Into New Habit:

The New Habit I Am Forming/Working On: | I Am Motivated By:

I Plan On Forming This New Habit Today By: | I Am Noticing:

I Am Letting Go Of The Old Feeling Of: | Despite How I Feel, I Will:

As I Start Working On My New Habit Today, I Will Feel: | I Look Forward To:

I Am Making Room For This New Habit In My Life By: | Today I Am Asking Myself:

Today I Will Set My Intention On: | The Answer To My Question Above Is:

I Am Maintaining The Positive Habits I Currently Have By:

A NEW WAY OF LIVING

Date: Mood: Days Into New Habit:

The New Habit I Am Forming/Working
On:

I Am Motivated By:

I Plan On Forming This New Habit Today
By:

I Am Noticing:

I Am Letting Go Of The Old Feeling Of:

Despite How I Feel, I Will:

As I Start Working On My New Habit
Today, I Will Feel:

I Look Forward To:

I Am Making Room For This New Habit In
My Life By:

Today I Am Asking Myself:

Today I Will Set My Intention On:

The Answer To My Question Above Is:

I Am Maintaining The Positive Habits I
Currently Have By:

A NEW WAY OF LIVING

Date: Mood: Days Into New Habit:

The New Habit I Am Forming/Working On:

I Am Motivated By:

I Plan On Forming This New Habit Today By:

I Am Noticing:

I Am Letting Go Of The Old Feeling Of:

Despite How I Feel, I Will:

As I Start Working On My New Habit Today, I Will Feel:

I Look Forward To:

I Am Making Room For This New Habit In My Life By:

Today I Am Asking Myself:

Today I Will Set My Intention On:

The Answer To My Question Above Is:

I Am Maintaining The Positive Habits I Currently Have By:

A NEW WAY OF LIVING

Date: Mood: Days Into New Habit:

The New Habit I Am Forming/Working On:

I Am Motivated By:

I Plan On Forming This New Habit Today By:

I Am Noticing:

I Am Letting Go Of The Old Feeling Of:

Despite How I Feel, I Will:

As I Start Working On My New Habit Today, I Will Feel:

I Look Forward To:

I Am Making Room For This New Habit In My Life By:

Today I Am Asking Myself:

Today I Will Set My Intention On:

The Answer To My Question Above Is:

I Am Maintaining The Positive Habits I Currently Have By:

TODAY I CELEBRATE....

MY RELEASED THOUGHTS

A NEW WAY OF LIVING

Date: Mood: Days Into New Habit:

The New Habit I Am Forming/Working On: I Am Motivated By:

I Plan On Forming This New Habit Today By: I Am Noticing:

I Am Letting Go Of The Old Feeling Of: Despite How I Feel, I Will:

As I Start Working On My New Habit Today, I Will Feel: I Look Forward To:

I Am Making Room For This New Habit In My Life By: Today I Am Asking Myself:

Today I Will Set My Intention On: The Answer To My Question Above Is:

I Am Maintaining The Positive Habits I Currently Have By:

A NEW WAY OF LIVING

Date: Mood: Days Into New Habit:

The New Habit I Am Forming/Working On:

I Am Motivated By:

I Plan On Forming This New Habit Today By:

I Am Noticing:

I Am Letting Go Of The Old Feeling Of:

Despite How I Feel, I Will:

As I Start Working On My New Habit Today, I Will Feel:

I Look Forward To:

I Am Making Room For This New Habit In My Life By:

Today I Am Asking Myself:

Today I Will Set My Intention On:

The Answer To My Question Above Is:

I Am Maintaining The Positive Habits I Currently Have By:

A NEW WAY OF LIVING

Date: Mood: Days Into New Habit:

The New Habit I Am Forming/Working On:

I Am Motivated By:

I Plan On Forming This New Habit Today By:

I Am Noticing:

I Am Letting Go Of The Old Feeling Of:

Despite How I Feel, I Will:

As I Start Working On My New Habit Today, I Will Feel:

I Look Forward To:

I Am Making Room For This New Habit In My Life By:

Today I Am Asking Myself:

Today I Will Set My Intention On:

The Answer To My Question Above Is:

I Am Maintaining The Positive Habits I Currently Have By:

A NEW WAY OF LIVING

Date: Mood: Days Into New Habit:

The New Habit I Am Forming/Working On:

I Am Motivated By:

I Plan On Forming This New Habit Today By:

I Am Noticing:

I Am Letting Go Of The Old Feeling Of:

Despite How I Feel, I Will:

As I Start Working On My New Habit Today, I Will Feel:

I Look Forward To:

I Am Making Room For This New Habit In My Life By:

Today I Am Asking Myself:

Today I Will Set My Intention On:

The Answer To My Question Above Is:

I Am Maintaining The Positive Habits I Currently Have By:

A NEW WAY OF LIVING

Date: Mood: Days Into New Habit:

The New Habit I Am Forming/Working On:

I Am Motivated By:

I Plan On Forming This New Habit Today By:

I Am Noticing:

I Am Letting Go Of The Old Feeling Of:

Despite How I Feel, I Will:

As I Start Working On My New Habit Today, I Will Feel:

I Look Forward To:

I Am Making Room For This New Habit In My Life By:

Today I Am Asking Myself:

Today I Will Set My Intention On:

The Answer To My Question Above Is:

I Am Maintaining The Positive Habits I Currently Have By:

WHAT I WILL BE DOING BETTER THIS TIME NEXT YEAR.....

A NEW WAY OF LIVING

Date: Mood: Days Into New Habit:

The New Habit I Am Forming/Working On:

I Am Motivated By:

I Plan On Forming This New Habit Today By:

I Am Noticing:

I Am Letting Go Of The Old Feeling Of:

Despite How I Feel, I Will:

As I Start Working On My New Habit Today, I Will Feel:

I Look Forward To:

I Am Making Room For This New Habit In My Life By:

Today I Am Asking Myself:

Today I Will Set My Intention On:

The Answer To My Question Above Is:

I Am Maintaining The Positive Habits I Currently Have By:

A NEW WAY OF LIVING

Date: Mood: Days Into New Habit:

The New Habit I Am Forming/Working On:

I Am Motivated By:

I Plan On Forming This New Habit Today By:

I Am Noticing:

I Am Letting Go Of The Old Feeling Of:

Despite How I Feel, I Will:

As I Start Working On My New Habit Today, I Will Feel:

I Look Forward To:

I Am Making Room For This New Habit In My Life By:

Today I Am Asking Myself:

Today I Will Set My Intention On:

The Answer To My Question Above Is:

I Am Maintaining The Positive Habits I Currently Have By:

A NEW WAY OF LIVING

Date: Mood: Days Into New Habit:

The New Habit I Am Forming/Working On: | I Am Motivated By:

I Plan On Forming This New Habit Today By: | I Am Noticing:

I Am Letting Go Of The Old Feeling Of: | Despite How I Feel, I Will:

As I Start Working On My New Habit Today, I Will Feel: | I Look Forward To:

I Am Making Room For This New Habit In My Life By: | Today I Am Asking Myself:

Today I Will Set My Intention On: | The Answer To My Question Above Is:

I Am Maintaining The Positive Habits I Currently Have By:

A NEW WAY OF LIVING

Date: Mood: Days Into New Habit:

The New Habit I Am Forming/Working On:	I Am Motivated By:
I Plan On Forming This New Habit Today By:	I Am Noticing:
I Am Letting Go Of The Old Feeling Of:	Despite How I Feel, I Will:
As I Start Working On My New Habit Today, I Will Feel:	I Look Forward To:
I Am Making Room For This New Habit In My Life By:	Today I Am Asking Myself:
Today I Will Set My Intention On:	The Answer To My Question Above Is:
I Am Maintaining The Positive Habits I Currently Have By:	

MY RELEASED THOUGHTS

A NEW WAY OF LIVING

Date: Mood: Days Into New Habit:

The New Habit I Am Forming/Working
On:

I Am Motivated By:

I Plan On Forming This New Habit Today
By:

I Am Noticing:

I Am Letting Go Of The Old Feeling Of:

Despite How I Feel, I Will:

As I Start Working On My New Habit
Today, I Will Feel:

I Look Forward To:

I Am Making Room For This New Habit In
My Life By:

Today I Am Asking Myself:

Today I Will Set My Intention On:

The Answer To My Question Above Is:

I Am Maintaining The Positive Habits I
Currently Have By:

A NEW WAY OF LIVING

Date: Mood: Days Into New Habit:

The New Habit I Am Forming/Working On:

I Am Motivated By:

I Plan On Forming This New Habit Today By:

I Am Noticing:

I Am Letting Go Of The Old Feeling Of:

Despite How I Feel, I Will:

As I Start Working On My New Habit Today, I Will Feel:

I Look Forward To:

I Am Making Room For This New Habit In My Life By:

Today I Am Asking Myself:

Today I Will Set My Intention On:

The Answer To My Question Above Is:

I Am Maintaining The Positive Habits I Currently Have By:

A NEW WAY OF LIVING

Date: Mood: Days Into New Habit:

The New Habit I Am Forming/Working On:	I Am Motivated By:
I Plan On Forming This New Habit Today By:	I Am Noticing:
I Am Letting Go Of The Old Feeling Of:	Despite How I Feel, I Will:
As I Start Working On My New Habit Today, I Will Feel:	I Look Forward To:
I Am Making Room For This New Habit In My Life By:	Today I Am Asking Myself:
Today I Will Set My Intention On:	The Answer To My Question Above Is:
I Am Maintaining The Positive Habits I Currently Have By:	

I AM FREE FROM OLD HABITS.

Made in the USA
Columbia, SC
03 December 2018